Australian Biographical Monographs

17

Australian Biographical Monographs

Series Editor: Scott Prasser

Previous Volumes

Australian Biographical Monographs

17

Robert (Bob) Hawke

Mike Steketee

Connor Court Publishing

Australian Biographical Monographs 17

Robert (Bob) Hawke by Mike Steketee
Published in 2022 by Connor Court Publishing Pty Ltd

Connor Court Publishing Pty Ltd
PO Box 7257
Redland Bay QLD 4165
sales@connorcourt.com
www.connorcourt.com
Phone 0497-900-685

Printed in Australia

ISBN:9781922815200

Front Cover Photo: Bob Hawke, Labor spokesman on industrial affairs and ACTU president, emphasises a point as he addresses a crowd at Victoria Square after leading the Labour Day procession down King William Street on Saturday, 11th October 1980. Photographer Jenny Scott.11 October 1980, 12:00:00, Flickr: Bob Hawke 1980, State Library of South Australia. Creative Commons Attribution 2.0, Generic license.

"It is difficult to see any Labor leader other than Hawke winning four consecutive elections, particularly given the economic turbulence of the 1980s and early 1990s."

\- Neal Blewett, Minister in the Hawke and Keating Governments.

The Connor Court Publishing's *Australian Biographical Series* on past leading Australian political leaders and other important figures seeks to provide an overview for those who are unfamiliar with the subject and to highlight the person's particular importance, controversies and contributions to Australia's progress.

The monographs are scholarly rather than academic in focus placing emphasis on a clear narrative, but with careful attention to referencing to ensure views expressed are supported by appropriate sources and evidence.

The Series was initiated because of the decline in the study of Australian history at our schools and universities and the consequential lack of knowledge or even worse, distorted views of some of Australia's leading figures who deserve to be remembered, understood for both their achievements, and as each volume also highlights, their flaws.

In this monograph journalist Mike Steketee provides a fresh assessment of the career of Bob Hawke. Widely regarded as one of Australia's best prime ministers, he won four successive elections between 1983 and 1990 – two more than any previous Labor prime minister and a record exceeded only by Robert Menzies, although equalled by John Howard. No prime minister has matched him for the sheer volume of major reforms, particularly on the economy. Some, such as the floating of the dollar in 1983, were heavily influenced by circumstances, many were a direct contradiction of traditional Labor policy and often they were driven by his brilliant but sometimes erratic Treasurer Paul Keating. But Hawke's political skills – what he called his special relationship with the Australian people – together with the strong role he played in leading a sometimes fractious government, produced successful government. Less attention has been paid to Hawke's substantial involvement in foreign policy and his reforms on social and environmental policies. And until recently still less attention was paid to aspects of Hawke's private life.

Mike Steketee was chief political correspondent for *The Sydney Morning Herald* in the Canberra Press Gallery from 1984 to 1988 and continued to cover the later years of the Hawke Government as the *Herald*'s Political Editor. It was an era when journalists abided by the longstanding convention that they should not report on the private lives of politicians unless it affected the way they performed their public duties. While it is widely known that Hawke stopped drinking for the period he was prime minister, fewer people realised until recently that he continued to have numerous sexual liasions while in office. Such behaviour, if it had become public, would have damaged him politically, perhaps fatally. Today it would disqualify him from becoming prime minister. Would Hawke have adapted to today's standards? Perhaps but we will never know definitely.

■ Scott Prasser (Series Editor)

Introduction

When Bob Hawke died in 2019, there was an outpouring of public emotion on a scale rarely seen for a politician. In the eyes of many Australians he had become a secular saint.

Some shed tears. Thousands gathered at the Sydney Opera House the following month for the memorial service and many more watched the live broadcast on television. One anonymous tribute captured the prevailing mood: "Good bloke, too".

Indeed, he was an uncommonly popular politician – a knockabout, sports loving larrikin who was a natural leader. He radiated authenticity – a precious and often elusive political commodity. Many Australians related to him as one of theirs. As Prime Minister he reached an approval rating of 78 per cent in March 1984 – a level unmatched before or since.

He had a formidable intellect but was too interested in the practical to ever be regarded as an intellectual – a species about which many Australians harbour suspicions. He was a celebrity politician, claiming a special relationship with the Australian people – one that Paul Keating, who succeeded him as prime minister, referred to derisively as "tripping over television cables in shopping centres". But it was a key to his, and Labor's, success.

Those close to Hawke rarely worshipped him in the way many members of the public did. Hawke had many attributes but, like all of us, he also had flaws. It is just that in his case they were writ large and they were more apparent to those who knew him best. He was vain to the point of narcissism. His life was an emotional roller coaster, including two occasions when he contemplated suicide. He was selfish and neglected his responsibilities as a husband and father. Voters knew that he liked a beer or three and had an eye for women and a typical reaction was "good for him". Fewer knew the extent to which he abused alcohol and that getting drunk could make him aggressive and obnoxious. Nor did most realise he was an incorrigible womaniser who, if he had lived 30 years later, would have risked multiple charges of sexual harassment. The most recent biography of Hawke, by Troy Bramston, describes him as a highly functioning alcoholic (before he became prime minister) and a sex addict (before and after).

Like any politician who aspired to reach the top, he was ruthless when he thought it advanced his interests, such as when he tore down Bill Hayden as Labor leader. Hawke once made the revealing comment that Kim Beazley, a senior member of his government, later Opposition Leader and the politician to whom he was closest, did not have enough "mongrel". It was not a quality he lacked.

But Hawke deserves credit for running one of the best federal governments Australia has seen. He presided over a series of courageous economic reforms that transformed Australia – the floating of the dollar, the deregulation of the financial system, the removal of tariff barriers, taxation and competition reform and some early steps on privatisation. Many were driven by his brilliant and mercurial Treasurer, Paul Keating, who advanced them further when he became Prime Minister through privatisation and labour market deregulation. It is a list of achievements all the more remarkable given the paucity of reforms subsequently. Hawke's popularity, authority and sometimes steadying hand played a large part in winning acceptance of the changes by the Labor Party and the public.

What has dimmed with time is how hard fought they were and how turbulent was their passage. None of them came naturally to a Labor government; in fact they mostly contradicted Labor policy and philosophy. They were triggered in part by circumstance and they were justified as a means to an end: creating a more prosperous Australia and one less prone to damaging recessions. They also were tempered by significant, and more characteristically Labor, reforms in social policy, such as the introduction of Medicare, directing welfare benefits to those most in need, including reducing child poverty, and universal superannuation.

The economic reforms tended to overshadow Hawke's active involvement in world affairs. While Australia ultimately has limited influence abroad, Hawke established the foundations for a strong economic relationship with China and played a leading role in ending apartheid in South Africa and banning mining in Antarctica.

When he won his third term in government in 1987, Hawke became his party's most successful federal leader. He went on to win a fourth term in 1990, making him, together with John Howard Australia's second most successful prime minister, as measured by election wins, after Robert Menzies. And then, the following year, he became the first Labor leader to be voted out of office by his party.

It was only one example of the vivid contrasts that marked his life and career. From an early age he seemed destined to become prime minister – he certainly thought so – but then spent years agonising over whether to enter federal parliament. Before he became Labor leader, he mixed hard work with a dissolute lifestyle that suggested to many he was unfit to lead the nation. Yet he was one of Australia's most successful prime ministers.

Early life and career

Hawke's biographer, Blanche d'Alpuget, who was to become his second wife, attributed his "unusually complex personality" to the stresses from bursting free of his upbringing in the narrowest of social enclaves – small town, fundamentalist Christianity. His father Clem was a Methodist, later Congregational, preacher and the family was living in Bordertown, South Australia, when Bob was born in 1929, on the eve of the Great Depression. Reconciling opposites became a theme in Hawke's life: in d'Alpuget's words, "hymn singer and boozer; family man and philanderer; mate of the manual worker and the millionaire".

She saw destiny at work from the start. His mother Ellie decided on the name Robert before he was born, aware of its popular meaning "of shining fame". When she was pregnant, taking out her Bible each day, she was astonished how often it fell open at the early chapters of Isaiah and how her eyes were drawn to the verse: "For unto us a child is born, unto us a son is given and the government shall be upon his shoulder". His father doted on him as a special child, particularly after the death of his older brother, Neil, from meningitis.

Whether or not there is a touch of literary licence here, Hawke himself certainly came to believe in his special talents, although the early years did not look promising. He was a sickly, small, thin child until Ellie took him at age 15 to a naturopath who changed his diet, which he attributes to his subsequent development into what one of his class mates recalled was a "real tough guy" who used to talk about how he was going to be prime minister.

After the family moved to Perth, Hawke won a scholarship to Perth Modern School, leaving in 1946 with an unexceptional pass, at least for a school with a reputation for outstanding students, and going on to the University of Western Australia to study law, as well as joining the Labor Club and the Student Christian Movement and playing first grade cricket. His uncle Albert, who was to become premier, had aroused his interest in politics.

At age 17, he had a motor bike accident that put him in hospital with a ruptured spleen and on the critical list for several days. Hawke told d'Alpuget it was a turning point: "I hadn't been using my talents, I hadn't taken school seriously; I hadn't taken university seriously. Lying there in hospital I decided I was going to live my life to my utmost ability, that I'd push myself to my limits". He graduated with second class honours, became president of the Guild of Undergraduates and went on to do a second degree in Arts and economics. In 1952, at his second attempt, he became a Rhodes Scholar.

A few weeks later he left to attend a world conference of Christian youth in India. The poverty and particularly the contrast with the relatively affluent lifestyle of his Christian brethren in India, came as a shock, leading him to the loss of his faith and becoming an agnostic. Seven months after his return, he left for Oxford.

Graham Freudenberg, speechwriter to successive federal Labor leaders, wrote that Hawke was "the only Australian to have left Oxford more convincedly Australian than before he went there". He made it into the Guinness Book of Records for drinking 2½ pints of beer in 12 seconds – a feat talked about, mainly admiringly, ever since. He chose as his thesis topic not a traditional or arcane academic subject but a treatise on Australia's Conciliation and Arbitration Commission.

Back in Australia, he married Hazel Masterson,

who he had met at church and was secretary of the Congregational Youth Fellowship when Hawke was president. Then they set out together for Canberra, where he had won a research scholarship at the Australian National University and wrote a thesis on the basic wage, leading to the offer of a job as a research officer at the ACTU. It was, writes d'Alpuget, an astonishing appointment for a trade union movement for which the words 'intellectual' and 'academic' often were pejoratives. But he quickly built a reputation for his advocacy in cases before the Conciliation and Arbitration Commission which, in the era before labour market deregulation, was the main vehicle for wage increases. As well, he was noted for his left wing views.

In 1953 the Commission had overturned 32 years of practice that had indexed the basic wage – the minimum legal income for an unskilled worker – to inflation. Instead, the wage would be increased only when the economy, or more precisely when business, was judged to have the capacity to pay. It was a major victory for employers. In 1959, it became Hawke's task as the ACTU advocate to persuade the Commission to reinstate indexation. He was aged 29 and unlike his predecessors, not a barrister even though he was appearing before a bench of three judges.

Hawke lectured and hectored and shouted his arguments – not a style that immediately appealed to judges used to deference and gentle persuasion from those appearing before them. But he eventually won them over by sheer logic and force of argument, backed by a knowledge of economics far greater than those on the bench. He produced evidence that productivity – output per worker – had increased by 10 per cent since 1953 and that therefore real wages should have risen by the same amount. Instead wages after inflation had fallen by 5 per cent since 1953. The bench refused to reinstate automatic indexation but agreed to increase the basic wage by 15 shillings, which represented a 17 per cent increase on the 1953 level – more than would have been delivered by indexation. A few weeks later, Hawke had another victory in a so called margins case, which reviewed the additional income for skills every five years and awarded a 28 per cent increase for the metal trades industry. Hawke had become a hero of the trade union movement. And he increasingly attracted broader attention from the media and the public – attention that he coveted and actively encouraged.

But Hawke also had his setbacks, such as in 1965 when the Commission refused to increase the basic wage and reverted to the capacity to pay formula. Hawke was criticised for mishandling the case and his aggressiveness before the judges, including referring to the "stupidity" of the tribunal at a previous hearing. "Along the Bench faces were pale with anger", wrote D'Alpuget. But it only seemed to put more fire in Hawke's belly, with his ego combining with a sense of righteous indignation. In the following year's case, his opening address lasted for three weeks and included a forensic demolition of the 1965 decision. The Commission awarded a $2 increase in the basic wage and reinstated the prices and productivity formula that the unions favoured.

In 1963, Hawke had made his first attempt to enter parliament, standing in the Victorian seat of Corio against Olympic cyclist and Menzies Government minister Hubert Opperman. He was reluctant to run but was persuaded by arguments about a sense of duty to the labour movement. In an election in which the national swing was to the Menzies Government, Hawke shifted votes towards him but not enough to win the seat. He subsequently regarded it as a lucky escape. "Who knows what 20 years in parliament, with all but three of them in opposition, would have done to my sense of what was possible for Australia in 1983?", he wrote in his biography. "Or what it would have done to me?" In 1966 Gough Whitlam, then deputy Labor leader to Arthur Calwell, tried unsuccessfully to persuade

Hawke to run again in Corio and when Whitlam became Opposition Leader after the election, made another attempt for the following election.

Hawke was ambitious but Labor had been out of office since 1949 and he was aiming to become ACTU president, a position of real power at a time when more than 50 per cent of employees belonged to a trade union, compared to 14 per cent in 2020. However, Hawke was a research officer who had never been in a 'real' job that involved union membership and he was running against Harold Souter, who had been secretary of the ACTU since 1957 and had the support of the dominant right wing on the ACTU executive. Hawke threw himself into a boots-and-all political battle, gaining the support of left-wing unions, including those led by Communists. When Souter warned about a "pro-Communist alliance front", Hawke countered with an attack on unions under the control of "the extreme Right wing, including the DLP". A split in the Labor Party in the 1950s had seen the formation of the Democratic Labor Party, which had Catholic roots, was strongly anti-Communist and directed its preferences to the Liberals – an important factor in keeping Labor out of power.

Hawke won the contest by a vote of 399 to 350. In the United States (US), George Meany, head of the ACTU's counterpart, the AFL-CIO, exclaimed: "The Aussies have gone Communist!" Hardly. Years later, when Hawke was in another pitched battle to enter federal parliament, the accusation from his opponents was that he was not a true Labor person, was a friend of capitalists such as Sir Peter Abeles and was altogether too right wing.

The following year, 1970, he met the director of an electrical store called Bourkes, Lionel Revelman, who offered Hawke an opportunity to expand a small, under-funded ACTU empire: a joint venture with Bourkes to tackle price fixing among big retail stores and a $3.5 million share of predicted future profits. The initiative, with its touch of a David and Goliath battle, attracted a flood of media and public interest to Hawke. When major manufacturers refused to supply stock to Bourkes, Hawke announced a union ban on moving goods to and from the Dunlop group of companies, which had taken the hardest line against Bourkes. Dunlop folded and, in a joint press conference with the company's chairman Eric Dunshea, Hawke announced the end of price fixing arrangements in Australia. Bourkes never generated the revenue promised for the ACTU and the business was wound up in the early 1980s. There were other joint ventures in travel and petrol stations that provided income for the ACTU for a period but

Hawke's grand vision of union businesses across the economy did not materialise. However, in terms of attracting public attention, he had done very well.

The reputation Hawke developed as a strike breaker further enhanced his national profile. At a time trade unions were far more powerful than today, union militancy threatened Labor's support just when it looked likely to win a federal election under Gough Whitlam. When Hawke intervened in disputes, usually only after they had escalated into major confrontations, he attracted a blaze of publicity. In the election year of 1972, he ended strikes in the power generation and oil industries.

Whitlam led Labor to power for the first time in 23 years in December 1972. Among Labor supporters there was elation and huge optimism about what the new government could deliver. More broadly there was acknowledgement that, as Labor's election slogan put it, "It's Time" for change. What was overlooked was that Labor's win against a government that had been in power for over two decades and was led by the hapless Billy McMahon was a relatively narrow one, with a majority of only nine seats.

In the first year of the Whitlam Government, Hawke became president of the Labor Party while remaining ACTU president. What might otherwise be regarded as a career-enhancing move turned out to be a poisoned chalice. The interests of the trade union movement and a Labor government do not always coincide. Sometimes they clash head on, such as when the government announced a 25 per cent cut in import tariffs across the board as an anti-inflationary measure. Wearing his two hats, Hawke made an unconvincing attempt to defend it while at the same time expressing concern about the workers who would lose their jobs.

Apart from that, Hawke found himself supporting a government that was rapidly losing public trust. Inflation was high and unemployment was rising, triggered by the quadrupling of international oil prices but exacerbated by the government's economic mismanagement. Whitlam won re-election in 1974, but only narrowly, after he called the Opposition's bluff over its threat to block the Budget. The following year, just as Bill Hayden as Treasurer was starting to bring the Budget under control, the Whitlam Government was overwhelmed by scandals, culminating in its momentous dismissal by Governor-General Sir John Kerr and its subsequent landslide defeat.

On the day after the election, Whitlam called Hawke to the Lodge in Canberra and offered him the leadership. There were a few technicalities, such as that Hawke did not have a seat in parliament and the position was not Whitlam's to bestow. Hawke made the mistake of saying publicly that Whitlam wanted him to take over, raising the hackles of the Labor Caucus, the body that elected the leader and of which Hawke was not even a member. The strongest criticism came from the Left, which Hawke increasingly had alienated. In any case, Whitlam soon changed his mind and decided he wanted to stay as leader.

In 1977, a defeat for Labor almost as bad as in 1975 saw Hayden replace Whitlam as leader. Hayden lacked the flair of Whitlam or the popular appeal of Hawke but he put the party back into the electoral race, with a substantial swing against the Fraser Government in the 1980 election. Nevertheless, the doubts about Hayden's leadership intensified the speculation about Hawke finally entering federal politics. The Victorian Socialist Left mounted a stop Hawke campaign, painting him as the stooge of big capitalism and Rupert Murdoch and a man who would betray Labor principles.

Hawke's own ambivalence raised questions about his suitability. In the words of d'Alpuget, "he was dying of indecision". When his party supporters lined up the numbers for him in the Melbourne seat of Wills in 1979, he decided not to run. Two weeks later he changed his mind and won preselection against the Left's candidate, Gerry Hand, later to become a minister in his government, by 38 votes to 29.

But that was not the end of it. He had admitted publicly on one occasion that he had a problem with alcohol but he continued drinking. His indiscretion, often but not solely when he was drinking, was notorious. In the bar outside Labor's 1979 national conference, Hawke, within earshot of journalists, unleashed a tirade against Hayden, calling him, amongst other things, "a lying c... with a limited future". It led to the impression of Hawke as an unguided missile and media predictions that he would never be leader. Nine months later, he swore off the grog. The repeated rumours that he had fallen off the wagon or inevitably would only fortified his determination to prove his critics wrong.

Hawke entered parliament at the 1980 election. In his first year in parliament, a Liberal MP accused him of abandoning Israel over Labor's opposition to an Australian contribution to a peacekeeping force in the Sinai. Hawke, whose support for Israel was deep-seated and emotional, fled the chamber in tears, making front page headlines and adverse comments about his toughness and stability. Appointed by Hayden as shadow minister for industrial relations, Hawke struggled to make an impact in parliament. He bristled over the arcane traditions of parliament, regarding most of the proceedings, with their pre-ordained outcomes governed by the party with the numbers, as a charade. His forte was the public meeting.

But the dissatisfaction with Hayden persisted. The following year, after a subterranean campaign that included Hawke's supporters leaking opinion poll findings reflecting badly on Hayden, the Opposition Leader called a meeting of Caucus and won a leadership ballot against Hawke by 42-37. Hayden survived but was weakened, making a second challenge inevitable - unless an election intervened.

A few months later d'Alpuget's biography of Hawke was published. Although an overwhelmingly favourable account, it was frank about his dissolute behaviour, including philandering and alcohol abuse. But rather than doing him further damage, it was like an act of redemption for Hawke: with his life, mostly warts and all, out in the open, it seemed there were few accusations about his personal life that could do him further harm. Moreover, many Australian men envied his lifestyle, if perhaps secretly. And while many women were less impressed with his behaviour, for others Hawke had a magnetic attraction.

For the Labor Party, it was somewhat similar. The federal parliamentary Labor Party, known as the Caucus, behaved like a club. Hawke was an outsider and resented by those, like Hayden and Paul Keating, who had worked long and hard to win elections. The Left revived the accusations that Hawke was not a true Labor person because of his association with rich businessmen and his support for policies such as uranium mining. But it was hard to ignore his electoral appeal.

It was a by-election in December 1982 in the Victorian seat of Flinders that sealed Hayden's fate. Flinders, which included the Mornington Peninsula, had long been a Liberal seat and it required a 5.5 per cent swing to change hands. It was close to the average swing in government-held seats in by-elections. Labor had been well ahead of the Coalition in opinion polls for most of 1982. Moreover, Australia was in deep recession, with unemployment reaching 10 per cent, while inflation was at 11 per cent. But Labor achieved a swing of less than three per cent. Malcolm Fraser had announced a national wage freeze during the by-election campaign, which provoked a split in

Labor ranks. Labor's candidate in the by-election was unimpressive. But inevitably the blame fell primarily on Hayden.

Labor had lost three successive elections and a new mood of pessimism descended on the party. Frantic behind-the-scenes activity culminated in a letter Labor Senator John Button, an astute and respected political figure who had been a close ally of Hayden, sent him on 28 January 1983 after unsuccessfully trying to persuade him to make a peaceful transition to Hawke. It summed up the mood of senior figures in the party. "You said to me that you could not stand down for a 'bastard' like Bob Hawke. In my experience in the Labor Party the fact that someone is a bastard (of one kind or another) has never been a disqualification for leadership of the party. It is a disability from which we all suffer in various degrees... I must say that even some of Bob's closest supporters have doubts about his capacities to lead the party successfully, in that they do not share his own estimate of his ability. The Labor Party is, however, desperate to win the coming election".

Six days later came one of the most extraordinary events in Australian political history. On February 3, Fraser, hoping to maintain the momentum generated by the Flinders by-election and fearful

that Labor could change leaders, went to see
Governor-General Sir Ninian Stephen to ask
for an early election. At the very same time but
without being aware of Fraser's decision, Hayden
announced his resignation to a meeting of shadow
cabinet. He had been convinced by Button's letter,
which he called "brutal but fair". Nevertheless, it
was a wrenching decision. "I am not convinced
that the Labor Party would not win under my
leadership", Hayden told the media. "I believe that
a drover's dog could lead the Labor Party to victory
the way the country is and the way the opinion
polls are showing up for the Labor Party".

But Fraser had been out-manoeuvred. When he
went to Government House, he was expecting
to fight an election against Hayden. When the
Governor-General granted him the election, his
opponent was Bob Hawke, although still to be
formally endorsed by the Labor Caucus five days
later.

With the economy in recession, a government
in its third term and Hawke's public popularity,
it required only a disciplined Labor campaign to
ensure victory. That was not quite the forgone
conclusion it seemed in retrospect, particularly
after Hawke reacted angrily to a question from
the ABC's Richard Carleton about whether

he had blood on his hands over the demise of Hayden. If voters had concerns about Hawke, they were whether he had the right temperament to be prime minister. The question touched a raw nerve in Hawke: political assassinations are never gentle affairs, however much Hawke might have pretended.

But he was a model of statesmanship and responsibility for the rest of the campaign. He exploited the recession and condemned what he argued was Fraser's divisive approach to government. He adopted Hayden's campaign themes of national recovery and reconstruction and added his own "r" - reconciliation. As well there were promises of a big spending program, tax cuts and petrol price reductions to tackle the recession. Fraser tried a scare campaign against Labor's "mad and extravagant promises", saying people's savings would be safer under their beds than in the bank. Hawke responded with a clever quip harking back to the 'reds under the beds' bogy that the Liberals had used against Labor in earlier times: "They can't put them under the bed because that's where the Commies are!"

Government and economic policy

On 5 March 1983, at the age of 53, after decades of frustration and a period of self-doubt, Hawke became prime minister. Labor's win was convincing: the two-party swing of 3.6 per cent came on top of the 4.2 per cent Labor had achieved under Hayden in 1980, resulting in a final Labor vote of 53.2 per cent – the highest vote it has ever received in a federal election. It gave the new government a majority of 25 in the 125-member House of Representatives, compared to the Whitlam Government's nine seat majority in 1972. It was all the more impressive considering that Labor had suffered a devastating loss in 1975 and some had questioned not only its legitimacy as a governing party but its very survival.

The day after the election, Treasury Secretary John Stone came to see Hawke and the new Treasurer Paul Keating with a reality check: the projected Budget deficit for 1983-84 was $9.6 billion. Adding Labor's election promises could take the figure up to $12 billion – the largest since World War Two. Hawke had received an inkling of the deficit figure before the election, leading him to qualify his election promises. It was the signal that the economy would come ahead of election promises and that pragmatism was the priority. In truth the

$9.6 billion figure was not a measure of anything tangible but a projection that Treasury typically calculated on pessimistic assumptions. But it was the excuse that Hawke and Keating used to abandon most of their promises on spending and tax cuts. And it was the political weapon that they used relentlessly to attack the Fraser Government's economic legacy.

From the very beginning, Hawke was intent on laying the foundations for something that had eluded federal Labor for all its history – long-term government – and with it the opportunity to entrench Labor policies - even, in his fondest hopes, to become the party of natural government. There was the lingering resentment that when Labor finally returned to power in 1972 after 23 years, its legitimacy had never been accepted, leading to breaches of convention such as the Coalition parties blocking the Budget and culminating in the sacking of Gough Whitlam by the Governor-General. But there also was a recognition of the failings of the Whitlam Government.

This is why Hawke drew an immediate and deliberate contrast with his Labor predecessor. In his victory speech on election night he promised not excitement or a great wave of reform but "calmness and a sense of assuredness". It did not sound like a revolution, socialist or otherwise, and that was precisely Hawke's intention. Determined not to allow a repeat of the indiscipline of the Whitlam Government, his first focus was process – the orderly management of government. Under Whitlam all ministers formed the Cabinet, meaning decision-making was unwieldy and sometimes resulting in those who lost in Cabinet appealing to Caucus to reverse the decision. Instead, Hawke created a Cabinet of 13 from the ministry of 27 elected by Caucus. Ministers, including those from the outer ministry who participated in Cabinet decisions in their area of responsibility, were required to support them in Caucus. In a strictly formal sense, the supremacy of the Labor Caucus in decision-making was preserved but in practice it was greatly weakened.

Another contrast was on foreign policy. Where Whitlam was intent on carving out a more independent foreign policy, sometimes at the cost of criticism from the US, Hawke went out of his way to build good relations with President Ronald Reagan and Secretary of State George Shultz, despite their conservative credentials. The Americans trusted Hawke and that was a political asset in Australia.

Third, Hawke drew a sharp distinction with

the Whitlam Government on economic policy. Whitlam had shown little interest in economics and it became one of his government's biggest liabilities. In many areas, Hawke left the running to his ministers, avoiding delving into the detail of policies unless there was a pressing political need to do so. But economic policy, together with foreign affairs, were exceptions. He had studied economics at university, prepared national wage cases for the ACTU, served on the Reserve Bank board for seven years as ACTU president and been a member of a committee of inquiry into manufacturing industry, headed by Gordon Jackson, the head of CSR.

Within a month of coming to government, Hawke presided over a national economic summit that brought together leaders in federal and state governments, business, unions and welfare and community groups. It was the epitome of Hawke's consensus approach. There was scepticism, including by some within the new government. The Opposition portrayed consensus as compromise when what was required was bold decision-making and characterised the Hawke approach as corporatism – those in positions of power stitching up the game for themselves. Significantly, the summit was held before the resumption of parliament and the venue was the House of Representatives chamber. The symbolism was clear: Hawke, no fan of parliament, was substituting the quest for agreement for the parliamentary clash that emphasised differences.

Hawke confronted the summit with "the gravest economic crisis in 50 years" and laid out his remedies: a Budget with a deficit of $8.5 billion and the Accord between the government and the ACTU. The Accord was a distinctive feature of Labor's economic policy, designed to subordinate wage increases to the overall demands of economic policy – in other words, to ensure that the kind of wage explosions that had occurred under both the Whitlam and Fraser governments and for which Hawke carried some responsibility as leader of the trade union movement, would not be repeated. It traded off part of the wage increases strong unions could achieve and that tended to flow on to the rest of the workforce under a centralised industrial system for the so-called social wage. This included universal health insurance under Medicare, more generous and targeted welfare benefits and compulsory superannuation. The Hawke Government's economic policy won endorsement from everyone present at the summit, with the sole exception of Queensland National Party Premier, Joh Bjelke-Petersen. The summit was also a success when it came to public opinion: voters liked the idea of community leaders agreeing on what was best for the country, rather than playing politics. In reality, there was plenty of politics involved; it was just that it was being played more subtly than usual. Within months of coming to government, Hawke's approval rating had shot up to 70 per cent.

The new government had luck on its side. The drought broke and this bolstered the economic recovery already underway. Hawke was blessed with an exceptionally strong team of ministers, including Keating as Treasurer, Gareth Evans as Attorney-General, Bill Hayden as Foreign Minister, John Button as Industry Minister and Neal Blewett as Health Minister. Others who made their mark later were Peter Walsh in Finance, Kim Beazley in Defence, John Dawkins in Education and Brian Howe in Social Security. In Cabinet, Hawke was a skilled chairman, letting ministers have their say and striving for consensus. His own working style was methodical and diligent.

Three days after the election the government had accepted Reserve Bank advice and devalued the dollar by 10 per cent, thought to be large enough to stop the damaging speculation in the currency. But almost immediately the dollar came under more pressure, as did the system under which officials set its value. In the first week of December, the

Reserve Bank spent $1.4 billion on buying foreign exchange to counter the overseas money flooding into the country. The Reserve Bank was advocating a free float of the dollar, as was Hawke's senior economic adviser Ross Garnaut. But Stone, the formidable Treasury Secretary, resisted, concerned about losing control of an instrument of economic policy and fearful that the Australian economy would be at the whim of international speculators. When Hawke concluded the lengthy internal debate by saying the dollar would be floated, Stone told him: "Prime Minister, you'll regret this; you'll come to see this as a terrible decision".

The float became the Hawke Government's most significant economic decision, exposing the economy to the full force of international competition. It was a step that had ramifications for most other aspects of economic policy. No longer could the exchange rate be used to cushion against inflation that was higher than overseas or to protect inefficient industries. Further steps towards financial deregulation removed the ceiling on interest rates and allowed foreign banks into Australia as a means of increasing competition. The latter was a controversial decision inside the Labor Party but Keating sold it with the same zeal and political skill that he had used to oppose it when John Howard as Treasurer had proposed it under the Fraser Government. The float and further financial deregulation triggered a wild ride during the 1980s, with the dollar crashing in value, a boom in credit, skyrocketing interest rates and big corporate failures culminating in a severe recession. Bob Johnston, the Reserve Bank Governor at the time, subsequently told the author Paul Kelly: "It's just as well they did not foresee all the consequences, otherwise we might not have got the change".

For a Labor government, it was a particularly bold decision, although one driven by circumstances, given the rapid growth of international currency markets trading in huge amounts of money.

In opposition, Labor had opposed the Fraser Government's first moves towards financial deregulation. Effectively subjecting economic policy to the whims of the free market was the very antithesis of Labor dogma. Many in the left of the party accused the government of selling out, seeing its actions as justifying the resistance they had shown to Hawke becoming leader.

It is easily forgotten how vehement were these complaints. In the early years of the government, Labor's national Left, a broader grouping than the parliamentary party but with Caucus members playing a prominent part, periodically held news conferences to criticise government decisions, particularly on economic policy. Stewart West, the only left wing member of the first Hawke Cabinet, resigned after eight months because he could not support a Cabinet decision on uranium mining. Brian Howe, a left wing minister outside Cabinet in the first term, accused the government on one occasion of having a "deficit fetish" and on another of policies that he compared to a mule – like the animal that cannot reproduce, they had no future. The Left took its grievances to Labor's national conferences which, in theory, were the supreme decision-making bodies of the party. The debates were robust and the votes close, with the government relying on the Right and Centre-Left factions carrying the day.

There was no denying that the Hawke Government was taking an overwhelmingly pragmatic rather than ideological approach. That was the instinct of Hawke and Keating and it coincided with a swing to deregulation and other conservative policies internationally with the election of Margaret Thatcher in the United Kingdom (UK) and Ronald Reagan in the US. Hawke could not claim to have a mandate for most of the economic decisions, since not only had there had been no inkling of them before the election, they often directly contradicted the policies Labor had espoused in opposition.

But Hawke and Keating were dominant in Cabinet and were strongly backed on economic decisions by Employment Minister Ralph Willis, Finance Minister John Dawkins and the fellow West Australian who succeeded him, Peter Walsh. This meant their authority was rarely challenged successfully by the full ministry or the Caucus, even though the Caucus had the final say on decisions. Science Minister Barry Jones asked Communications Minister Michael Duffy on one occasion after an economic policy announcement following a meeting of the full ministry: "How did that happen?" "It's purely a matter of numbers," Duffy replied. "There's four of them and only 23 of us".

The Hawke Government had another advantage: on the hardest economic decisions, such as the float, financial deregulation more broadly and in subsequent years cutting tariffs, privatisation and labour market deregulation, it had the support of the Opposition, particularly that of John Howard, first as shadow treasurer and from 1985 as leader. All these decisions were in line with the philosophy of the Liberal Party or at least that of its conservative wing led by Howard, who had tried unsuccessfully to persuade the Fraser Government to adopt some of the same measures.

Over time, the dissension in the ranks reduced, though it still flared up from time to time. In his second term, Hawke appointed Howe to Cabinet's Expenditure Review Committee, which took all the main decisions on the spending side of the Budget. It brought Howe inside the tent and confronted the Left with difficult decisions: the constraint imposed by the imperative of reducing the Budget deficit meant that increased spending on new or existing programs, such as in Howe's area of welfare, had to be offset by other savings.

One of Hawke's underrated achievements was the skill he brought to decision-making, particularly on contentious issues. He would come to Cabinet meetings well briefed but would first listen patiently to his Ministers, making them feel their contributions were valued. Then he would sum up the debate and conjure up a solution to what sometimes seemed intractable issues – one that satisfied most of the concerns or, if not, that his colleagues felt they could live with.

Apart from economic policy, there were other areas where Hawke was intent on winning the trust of conservatives. Historically, Labor had had an antagonistic relationship with ASIO, the Australian Security Intelligence Organisation which was the domestic spy agency. In particular, the connections of some left wing Labor figures with the Communist Party had attracted ASIO's attention. In April 1983, barely a month after the election of the new government, ASIO Director-General Harvey Barnett came to see Hawke to tell him that a Soviet diplomat, Valeri Ivanov, whom ASIO had bugged after identifying him as a KGB agent, was cultivating a close relationship with David Combe, the former national secretary of the ALP. Combe, who also happened to be a close friend of Hawke's, was keen to use his influence with the new government in his new career as a lobbyist. Hawke immediately saw the implications of a spy scandal that would revive concerns over Labor's credentials on national security.

With Hawke leading the way, the government expelled Ivanov and banned Combe's access to ministers, effectively ruining his new found business. Mick Young, a member of Cabinet's security sub-committee, had mentioned the decision on Ivanov's expulsion to his friend and lobbyist, Eric Walsh, prompting Hawke to sack Young as Special Minister of State. Young, a former shearer with a knockabout manner and acute political skills, was another close mate of Hawke's. "Demanding Mick's resignation was the hardest thing I had to do in government," Hawke wrote in his autobiography.

Hawke's actions, though ultimately backed by Cabinet, attracted strong criticism from within the party. It was seen by many as an over-reaction and confirmed the Left's suspicion of Hawke as too willing to pander to conservative forces. Here was a Labor prime minister bending to the wishes of an organisation that had long been Labor's enemy. It was a perception reinforced by examples of mistakes and sloppy work by ASIO on the case, feeding into a sense that Combe and Young had been treated unfairly. Hawke ultimately claimed vindication from a Royal Commission, which found the government's actions justified. It neutralised the politics of what had threatened to be a first class security scandal. But it came at a cost, particularly to Combe's reputation, despite his protestations of innocence.

Years later Bramston revealed that Barnett had briefed Hawke on another security concern: that one of his ministers, Senator Arthur Gietzelt, had been, and still could be, an undercover member of the Communist Party while also a member of the Labor Party. That too would have caused a sensation had it come out in public at the time, even though the Communist Party had long since ceased being a threat in Australia. The Labor Caucus had elected

Gietzelt to the ministry, meaning that Hawke had to give him a portfolio unless he sacked him. He made the judgement that Gietzelt's Communist links would have no impact on his position as Minister for Veterans Affairs.

Enjoying an extended honeymoon in the opinion polls and wanting to avoid separate elections for the House and Senate, Hawke decided to go to the people in December 1984, only 21 months after the 1983 victory. Labor strategists were counting on a repeat of Neville Wran's success for Labor as NSW Premier, when he followed up his narrow victory in 1976 with two 'Wranslides' in 1978 and 1981, setting the party up for long-term government. But Hawke was over-confident. He opted for an unusually long campaign of seven-and-a half weeks in the expectation that he could destroy his Liberal opponent, Andrew Peacock. Instead, he gave him a platform as alternative prime minister. As well, Hawke campaigned poorly. He broke down in tears at a news conference over the heroin addiction of his daughter. Wracked with guilt over the neglect of his parental duties, "I was within minutes of resigning from office at that time", he said later.

Rather than destroying his opponent, Peacock proved to be an effective campaigner, hammering away day after day to get a plain message across to voters: that, "as certain as night follows day", a re-elected government would bring in new taxes. Peacock based his claim on reforms introduced in Labor's first term – an assets test on the aged pension and a 30 per cent tax on lump sum superannuation, both of which he promised a Liberal government would repeal. Labor's defence was muddied by Hawke's off-the-cuff commitment during a radio interview to hold a tax summit after the election. It meant Labor could deflect questions about the specifics of tax changes until after the election but at the same time it added ammunition to the Liberals' scare campaign. But Hawke emphasised another commitment: that under a second-term Labor government there would be no overall increase in taxation as a proportion of national income (GDP) and the same would apply to government expenditure and the Budget deficit. The so-called trilogy became a means of enforcing harsh discipline in future budgets. But in the election campaign voters were more inclined to believe their taxes would be going up than that Labor would keep its promise.

Not for the first time, the result of the 1984 election defied predictions of a thumping victory for Labor. Instead of a swing to Labor, the Opposition gained 1.46 per cent in the vote after preferences, cutting

Labor's majority from 25 seats to 16. With 51.8 per cent of the vote after preferences, it was a solid win for Labor but, given expectations of a landslide, it was the Liberals who were celebrating – except for Howard, who had expected to become Opposition Leader after the election loss. As for Hawke, the political messiah had been reduced to a mere mortal.

The tax summit held in July 1985 led to the most significant reforms to the tax system since World War Two, when the Curtin Government took over income tax from the states. Given there are few things more difficult in politics than bringing in new taxes, it was an enormous achievement. But the reforms were hard won and caused strains within the government and particularly between Hawke and Keating. Treasury produced a 280-page White Paper that canvassed options while convincing its minister of the case for big bang reform, referred to as Option C – taxes on capital gains and fringe benefits, including business lunches and entertainment allowances, with a trade-off in lower income taxes, and a 12.5 per cent consumption tax, equivalent to today's GST. In 23 hours of debate over three days and despite vociferous opposition, Keating won Cabinet endorsement to take the package, complete with consumption tax, forward to the summit as the government's preferred position.

That in itself was a remarkable piece of successful advocacy, since such a consumption tax broke a core Labor principle – it was regressive, hitting lower income earners harder because they consumed more and saved less than the better off. The argument in favour was that it would make tax collection more efficient, take some of the burden off income tax and that its regressive nature could be neutralised by compensation paid to low income earners, including those on welfare benefits. But just how contrary it was to Labor principles was epitomised in the 1993 election, when Keating as prime minister, with just as much zeal and apparent conviction as when he put the opposite argument in 1985, campaigned against Opposition Leader John Hewson's policy of a consumption tax. It was a major factor, though not the only one, in Hewson losing the so called 'unloseable' election. John Howard had favoured such a tax when he was Treasurer in the Fraser Government but made little headway in convincing his colleagues. After having promised before the 1996 election to "never, ever" bring it in, he eventually claimed a mandate in his second term and a GST was introduced in 2000.

But in 1985 Keating could not clear the final hurdle – the endorsement of the tax summit, where a consumption tax was opposed by trade unions, business, welfare groups and Labor premiers. Hawke, who also had been unenthusiastic about it, announced its demise at the summit over a bitterly resentful Keating, who in private called Hawke "old jellyback". In his biography Hawke justified pulling the plug by writing: "If I had not dumped Option C in 1985, Labor would have lost the 1987 election".

What was left was a major package of tax reform: a capital gains tax, a fringe benefits tax, a clampdown on other tax shelters, a reduction in the top income tax rate from 60 per cent to 49 per cent and the 46 per cent rate to 40 per cent, increasing the company tax rate from 46 per cent to 49 per cent and dividend imputation, which meant ending the double taxation of dividends. There was debate within Labor over whether the reforms were progressive – certainly there were few direct benefits for low to middle income earners. For higher income earners, the opportunities for minimising their tax were reduced through the new taxes on capital gains and fringe benefits, with a trade-off through a lower top rate of tax and dividend imputation.

There was scepticism, including within the government, about Hawke's penchant for summitry, with the critics arguing that it was the government's job to make decisions. But Hawke used this brand of consensus politics to win support for government decisions, as with economic policy in 1983, or, in the case of the consumption tax, to use the lack of community support to kill it off.

That is not to say that the remaining tax changes were popular. The Coalition was convinced that it would win the next election by opposing the new taxes and in different circumstances it may well have. Hawke, with Keating's encouragement, called an unusual mid-winter election in July 1987 to take advantage of disarray in conservative politics. Queensland Premier Joh Bjelke-Petersen, buoyed by victories in state elections and with the support of figures on the far Right, decided he wanted to be prime minister, splitting the National Party and breaking up the federal Coalition in the process. John Howard, who had succeeded Andrew Peacock as Opposition Leader in 1985, went to the election with a policy of huge income tax cuts, together with the scrapping of most of the government's tax reforms. Labor branded the policy as profligacy and revived the age-old campaign line usually deployed against Labor of "where's the money coming from?" That became a much more potent criticism when Treasury found a mistake in the calculations that Keating argued would cost the Budget an extra

$1.6 billion. Howard had to concede the basic point that there had been a double counting error but claimed the cost was $534 million. Hawke campaigned on responsible government, making few major promises, and labelled the Coalition economic vandals.

Despite the disruption of Bjelke-Petersen's quixotic campaign, the doubt about the Coalition's economic credibility and Hawke's instinctive appeal to voters, Labor secured only a narrow victory. The Coalition actually won a higher share of the primary vote – 46 per cent versus Labor's 45.8 per cent – but after the distribution of preferences, Labor prevailed by the narrowest of margins – 50.8 per cent to 49.2 per cent. Labor did much better in terms of seats, with a swing towards it in Queensland enabling it to pick up four more seats and increase its lower house majority from 16 to 24. It was an historic achievement for Hawke and Labor: the first time a Labor government had won a third term.

Also influencing the 1987 election was the drop in living standards Australians had suffered as a result of a decline in the terms of trade – the price we receive for our exports compared to the cost of imports. This was caused largely by a fall in international prices for commodities that was outside the government's control but to which it had to respond. It was reflected in a 40 per cent drop in the value of the dollar, making exports more competitive but imports more expensive, which in turn fed into higher inflation. It meant, said the Hawke Government, that Australia was living beyond its means. The issue had come to a head in May 1986 when Keating in a radio interview with broadcaster John Laws indulged in hyperbole, saying that if "Australia is so undisciplined, so disinterested in its salvation and its economic wellbeing that it doesn't deal with these fundamental problems...then you are gone; you are a banana republic".

Keating admitted later that he had gone too far in what were off-the-cuff comments but the words had a dramatic effect. The Treasurer had announced that Australia faced an economic crisis and the dollar immediately fell three cents. Hawke, in Tokyo on his way to Beijing, was furious and his mood got worse when Keating announced a special meeting of government, employers and unions – described by the media as a summit – to address the crisis. Stung particularly by commentary that it was Keating, not he, who was really running the country – a view that Keating was only too happy to encourage – Hawke gave the travelling media corps a background briefing in Beijing to send the message that he was reasserting control. He said the Deputy Prime Minister, Lionel Bowen, would chair the special meeting, not Keating, and it would be the government that made decisions, not the meeting. The next day he talked to senior ministers in a telephone hook-up to emphasise the point about who was in control. The episode further strained the relationship between Hawke and Keating. The Treasurer's remarks had been politically damaging but they reset the debate, focusing the government and the community on the severity of the economic situation. They paved the way for substantial cuts in government spending and agreement by the ACTU under the Accord to limit wage claims. They were steps in returning the Budget to surplus in 1987-88 for the first time since before World War Two, followed by three more surpluses.

The banana republic warning did something more: it brought home the extent to which the economy was subject to international market forces. If the Hawke Government did not respond, then the floating dollar would. It led to the era of micro-economic reform, removing the tariff protection that shielded many Australian industries from import competition and reforming the airline and telecommunications industries to make them more competitive. This was the agenda for the third and fourth terms of the Hawke Government. It also included the sale of public assets in the name of greater efficiency but Hawke, for all his standing as Labor's most successful prime minister, could not bring the party with him. That was left to the Keating Government, as was moving from centralised decision-making in the labour market to bargaining at the enterprise level and further reforms to increase competition.

But Hawke, Keating and Industry Minister John Button did succeed on tariffs, a particularly challenging issue for Labor since it threatened the jobs of many trade union members. The Whitlam Government had cut tariffs across the board by 25 per cent and suffered the political consequences, including a huge swing against it in a by-election in 1975 in the Tasmanian seat of Bass, which had a textile industry that benefited from high tariffs. As with the Hawke Government's broader economic policy, once more pragmatism and economic imperatives prevailed over Labor dogma. Hawke called it slaughtering sacred cows. From 1988 tariffs were gradually reduced across manufacturing, affecting particularly the car industry and textiles, clothing and footwear, which employed hundreds of thousands of people but were inefficient by international standards and meant Australian consumers paid high prices for their products. Tariff cuts were another example where Labor benefited from the support of the Opposition, for whom it meant forgoing the tempting political opportunity to exploit the fear of job losses.

There was another consequence of financial deregulation: a severe recession in 1990. Tight fiscal policy had brought the Budget into surplus in 1988 and Keating did not want to make more cuts to slow down what had become an economic boom. Instead, he relied on monetary policy – raising interest rates to slow down demand. Keating took credit for interest rate policy, saying the Reserve Bank "do as I say", which was not the reality but became a political liability as ever-increasing rates took their toll. Interest rates of 18 per cent and higher triggered the collapse of businesses, as well as pain for households with mortgages, and in 1992, unemployment reached 11.1 per cent, higher than the recession the government had inherited from the Fraser Government and the highest level since the Great Depression in the 1930s. Keating tried to make the best of it in November 1990 by calling it the "recession that Australia had to have". He meant it was necessary to squeeze inflation out of the system and to bring the external trade accounts back into balance but it was lethal political ammunition for the Coalition.

It was Labor's good fortune that Hawke had called an election in March 1990, when interest rates had started coming down and before the economy went into recession. Nevertheless, given the hardship high interest rates had caused, including business collapses, and the fact that the government was seeking a fourth term, there was considerable pessimism in Labor ranks about its prospects. Hawke's opponent was Andrew Peacock, who had replaced Howard in a surprise coup the year before and had proven himself to be an effective campaigner in the 1984 election. While there was voter disillusionment with Labor, there also were doubts whether Peacock had enough substance to be a successful prime minister – a sentiment captured by Keating's barb: "Can a souffle rise twice?" Labor in effect conceded it would lose votes by making a direct appeal for the second preferences of those not voting Labor, putting forward its superior credentials, particularly on the environment, at a time of heightened concern over this issue. It was a risky strategy but it turned out to be a winning one, with the Australian Democrats, other minor parties and independents receiving 17 per cent of the vote. While Labor's primary vote fell 6.4 percentage points below its 1987 result to 39.4 percent, well behind the Coalition's 43.5 per cent, Labor gained the lion's share of the preferences. That still left it behind the Coalition but only just, 49.9 per cent to 50.1 per cent. Labor lost ten seats, nine of them in Victoria which, after accounting for an electoral redistribution, reduced its majority to eight. It was fortunate, as it had been in 1987, in limiting the swing against it in its marginal seats. Hawke had bolstered his standing as Labor's greatest election winner but the 1990 election was another example of how fine was the line between long-term Labor government and a return to opposition.

Social and environmental policies

The largest social reform enacted by the Hawke Government was the introduction of Medicare. Its predecessor, Medibank, had been implemented in the last year of the Whitlam Government in 1975 over the strident opposition of doctors and the Coalition parties, who decried it as nationalised medicine. Australia was one of the last developed countries apart from the US to introduce a system of universal national health insurance. The Fraser Government set out to systematically dismantle Medibank but, despite five major changes in eight years in office, it never settled on a viable policy. The Hawke Government had fewer problems than its Labor predecessor. Despite another forthright campaign against it by the Australian Medical Association, Medicare began operating in February 1984. It took another 12 years before the Opposition came to fully accept it, with John Howard promising in his successful 1996 election campaign to continue Medicare, despite his promises in the 1987 election to pull it "right apart". Howard's fundamental view had not changed: his stance was a triumph of pragmatism over ideology. Not only was Medicare publicly popular but it did not have the dire consequences predicted for it of unsustainable health spending, let alone the 'enslavement' of doctors.

On welfare, the Hawke Government used means testing to concentrate benefits to those most in need, starting with an assets test on the age pension in 1984. Hawke made his most significant commitment on welfare during the campaign for the 1987 election through a family allowance supplement aimed at 500,000 low income families, including one million children. Labor's policy document said it would mean that "no child will need to live in poverty" but in his campaign policy speech, Hawke indulged in hyperbole by saying that "by 1990 no Australian child will be living in poverty". It became one of Hawke's most infamous promises, attracting ridicule and detracting from what was a major initiative. The child poverty package increased family payments and extended them from families without paid work to low paid working families. According to research by the National Centre for Social and Economic Modelling (NATSEM), this resulted in a one-third drop in child poverty between 1982 and 1996. In 1988 the government introduced another important measure to address poverty amongst single parents and their children. Concerned about separated and divorced parents avoiding their responsibilities, the Child Support Scheme collected and enforced maintenance payments, including through the garnisheeing of incomes by the Australian Taxation Office. It was recognised internationally as an innovative solution.

The Hawke Government increased spending on school education and directed more of the funding to poorer schools, as well as introducing programs to encourage students to complete Year 12. Retention rates doubled to nearly 80 per cent during the Hawke Government's four terms, although it is likely some of this increase would have occurred in the absence of specific measures.

More controversially, the Hawke Government re-introduced fees for university students. One of the more popular decisions of the Whitlam Government had been free university education.

But it had done little to achieve one of its objectives: increasing the numbers of people from lower income households going to university. John Dawkins, Education Minister in the third Hawke Government, introduced the Higher Education Contribution Scheme (HECS). Fees were imposed but they were not required to start being repaid until students earned income above a specified level. The argument was that university graduates on average enjoyed higher incomes and should be required to make a contribution to their tertiary education, rather than the whole burden falling on general taxpayers, including those on lower incomes unlikely to go to university. HECS has continued to arouse opposition, particularly from students, but it has been retained by successive governments.

Hawke established his credentials on the environ-ment with one of the first acts of his government, using the Constitution's external affairs power to override a Tasmanian Government decision to build a dam on the Franklin River. Though this pledge in the 1983 campaign contributed to Labor failing to win any of the five seats in Tasmania, it was a popular decision in the rest of Australia. In the 1987 election Hawke promised to protect the rainforests of North Queensland by placing them on the list of World Heritage sites – a pledge fulfilled after the election despite a bitter fight with the Queensland Government, the timber industry and timber workers, including a physical assault on Environment Minister Graham Richardson. Richardson negotiated a $75 million compensation package for timber workers who lost their jobs. The boundaries of the Great Barrier Reef Marine Park were extended. In 1988 the Hawke Government nominated a large area of the southern Tasmanian forests for World Heritage listing. No doubt attracted by an example of consensus politics, Hawke accepted a joint proposal by the Australian Conservation Foundation and the National Farmers' Federation to establish Landcare, which has played an important role in repairing damaged land and rivers. These decisions gave the government a decidedly green tinge, which served it well in the 1990 election.

In 1991 Hawke lent his strong support to Richardson and against the objections of other senior ministers to extend Kakadu National Park to block a BHP mine at Coronation Hill. Hawke called it "the most intense and bitter Cabinet debate in my whole time in government". Hawke invoked the spiritual beliefs of the indigenous people in the area in their opposition to the mine. Typically in Cabinet meetings Hawke allowed ministers to state their case and for the debate to flow before intervening or summing up at the end. On this occasion he led the debate, spoke passionately and prevailed even though the majority of Cabinet favoured economic development and opposed his stance but were not prepared to defeat him. Hawke writes in his autobiography that he was prepared to resign over the issue if he did not get his way.

Hawke also fought opponents in Cabinet, as well as governments overseas, over his insistence on banning mining and drilling for oil in the Antarctic, even though it had been provided for in a draft convention. He mounted a diplomatic campaign that included lobbying leaders in France, Britain and the US, culminating in countries agreeing to a ban on resource exploration, mining and oil drilling. The comment was often made, including by his colleagues, that Hawke had few strong beliefs. But there were exceptions.

One area that Hawke was not prepared to put his reputation on the line was indigenous land rights. A promise for national land rights legislation was dropped after objections by the mining industry and the Western Australian Premier, Brian Burke. In 1988, he promised a treaty with Aboriginal and Torres Strait Islander people. That too did not proceed. But the Government did hand back Ayers Rock or Uluru to its traditional owners and established the Aboriginal and Torres Strait Islander Commission (ATSIC) that was elected by indigenous people and administered government programs, giving indigenous people a degree of self-determination. It was seen widely as failing to live up to its promise and was abolished by the Howard Government following allegations of corruption and other controversies.

Susan Ryan, the only woman in Cabinet and the first from the Labor Party, introduced the Sex Discrimination Act, making it illegal to discriminate on the grounds of sex, marital status or pregnancy, including in employment. It was followed with legislation requiring larger employers to introduce affirmative action programs. There was a substantial expansion of government-subsidised child care from 1985.

Foreign Affairs

Like many prime ministers but often more so, Hawke became increasingly absorbed in foreign affairs – a subject to which he devoted several hundred pages of his 618-page biography. One of the arguments he used to convince himself and others that he should stay as prime minister and not succomb to leadership pressure from Keating was that he had established credentials and contacts that enabled him to play a more important role in world affairs. Apart from anything else, international visits were a welcome relief from the often petty politics of Canberra.

There are limits to what a middle power like Australia can achieve on the world stage. This did not stop Hawke trying and he built substantial relationships with world leaders. He found his authority challenged in 1985 over an agreement with the Reagan Administration for American aircraft to use an RAAF base to monitor tests of a new generation of intercontinental ballistic missiles, the MX, with a planned splashdown in the Tasman sea. Labor policy was to oppose the development and testing of new missile systems that contributed to the arms race. Hawke had a different priority: to cultivate good relations with the US, despite its deeply conservative Administration, and thereby overcome another bogey dating back to the Whitlam Government – the concern in Washington that a Labor government could not be trusted on defence and national security. Hawke had consulted with Foreign Minister Bill Hayden and Defence Minister Gordon Scholes but the rest of the government was caught by surprise when the journalist Brian Toohey revealed the agreement in the *National Times*. Hawke was in Brussels on a trip scheduled to take him to Washington when Graham Richardson, former NSW party secretary, now a Senator and a supporter of Hawke, rang to brief him on the spreading outrage in the party and advised him to back down. Facing a large scale revolt by his MPs and concerned about re-opening old wounds about the American alliance, Hawke agreed, requiring him to prostrate himself before the US Secretary of State, George Shultz, who he counted as a friend and who promptly withdrew the request for Australian help.

On many issues, Hawke's role inevitably was peripheral, however much he fancied himself as a player on the world stage. On his trip to the Soviet Union in 1987 he developed a rapport with Mikhail Gorbachev, who not long before had introduced the policies of liberalisation called perestroika and glasnost. A meeting scheduled for 20 minutes continued for more than 3 hours. "I still look back on that meeting as one of the most important, and certainly most fascinating, of my prime ministership", Hawke wrote in his autobiography. He sent a five-page letter on his discussions to US President Ronald Reagan. Hawke did not claim he was changing the course of human history with such interventions but called it "a useful and routine part of international dialogue".

One of the issues he raised with Gorbachev was the release of dissident Soviet Jews, known as 'refuseniks', who had been jailed or refused exit visas. Hawke's support for Israel was deep-seated, emotional and went back to his days as trade union leader. "I think the most emotional experience of my whole career was a meeting with Golda Meir, the Israeli Prime Minister in 1973", Hawke wrote. She wept in front of Hawke, blaming herself for the deaths of 2500 young Israelis in the Yom Kippur war. At her request, he went to the Soviet Union to argue for the release of 'refuseniks'. In 1979, during his third visit, he received assurances that some would be allowed to emigrate but the Soviets reneged in what Hawke described as an act of "vicious duplicity". Devastated, he remembered the joy in the eyes of the 'refuseniks' when he had told them of their imminent release and imagined the despair they would now be feeling. It led him to contemplate suicide. In 1987 he gave Gorbachev a list of six 'refusenik' cases and asked for their release. Gorbachev bristled at the request but on the morning of Hawke's departure, he was told two families would be released and the following year more of those whom Hawke had met in Moscow were allowed to emigrate as part of a broader easing of restrictions on Soviet Jews.

Hawke put great effort into building the

relationship with China, with three visits in four years and two visits to Australia by Chinese leaders. As with the Soviet Union, it was a time of enormous change, with the ascension of Deng Xiaoping in 1978 heralding the opening of the Chinese economy. He spent many hours in talks with Premier Zhao Ziyang and party secretary Hu Yaobang, whom he described as "a complete extrovert". In 1985 Hawke accompanied Hu to the Pilbara in Western Australia, resulting in China entering into a joint venture in the Mount Channar iron ore mine. Together with a 10 per cent stake in the Victoria's Portland aluminium smelter, they were China's biggest overseas investments at the time. They paved the way for China becoming Australia's largest trading partner.

Needless to say, the circumstances of the Chinese-Australian relationship were very different from the present day. Hawke received a foretaste of the future with the brutal repression of demonstrators in Tiananmen Square in 1989. At a memorial service in Parliament House commemorating the victims of the massacre, Hawke wept as he spoke. He made the unilateral decision, without Cabinet consultation, to allow the more than 40,000 Chinese students in Australia to stay indefinitely. Both Hu and Zhou were deposed as the hardliners in China reasserted control. But Hawke retained his optimism about China's future, including that political liberalisation would "inevitably" follow economic reforms. On that he has been proven wrong, at least for the forseeable future.

Hawke took the initiative in 1989 to bring together countries in our broad region in a grouping called APEC – Asia Pacific Economic Co-operation. He saw it as a means of increasing economic inter-dependence and lowering trade barriers – what he called "enmeshing" the economies in the region. Initial members were the US, Japan, South Korea, Australia, New Zealand and the then six ASEAN countries – Indonesia, Malaysia, Singapore, the Philippines, Thailand and Brunei. Keating as Prime Minister played a critical role in elevating APEC meetings to heads of government level.

Hawke used Australia's membership of the Commonwealth of Nations to push for stronger action to end apartheid in South Africa. On top of sanctions previously imposed that had done little to change South African policies, he proposed financial measures to cut off overseas investment in South Africa – a scheme that was adopted by Commonwealth heads of government in Kuala Lumpur in 1989 despite the strident objections of British Prime Minister Margaret Thatcher. It was a factor in the decision of the new South African

President, F.W. de Klerk, to end apartheid and free Nelson Mandela after 27 years in prison. Mandela subsequently gave credit to Hawke for his role in hastening the collapse of the old order.

In 1991, Hawke took Australia to war in the Middle East. The first Gulf war was triggered by Iraq under Saddam Hussein invading neighbouring Kuwait, an oil-rich state. Australia supported an immediate decision by the United Nations Security Council to impose sanctions on Iraq, which mostly affected Australian wheat sales. Our sanctions were enforced by sending two frigates and a support ship to the Gulf. When the sanctions proved ineffective in persuading Saddam to leave Kuwait, the US sent military forces to drive Iraq out and Hawke sent a team of mine clearance divers to help protect shipping.

In deciding to send a military force, Hawke was invoking an Australian tradition followed by both sides of politics and stretching back to the Menzies Government. In short, it ingratiated itself with the US. Before Australia sent troops to Vietnam in 1965 to support the American war effort, the Government arranged for South Vietnam to ask for an Australian contribution. Bramston reveals that Hawke did something similar by suggesting to US President George H.W. Bush that he ask for

Australian assistance. According to the transcripts of phone calls, Hawke rang Bush and said: "For presentation, you called me, we had a yarn... We indicated our willingness to be part of it". Bush agreed: "We will say that I called you to request if Australians could participate. You were positive". At a news conference the same day, Hawke lied by saying the phone call had come from Bush, not the other way around. He then announced that Australia would send the three ships to the Gulf.

"The Gulf War was in many ways the most demanding single challenge I dealt with in my public life," Hawke wrote in his biography. It is a reminder that decisions to send Australians to war without knowing the consequences weigh heavily on leaders. In the event the US took less than five days to drive Iraqi forces back to Baghdad. Australia suffered no casualties. A by-product of the war was that it boosted Hawke's standing as prime minister at the very time that Keating was stalking him. But it only delayed the Keating challenge.

Keating strikes

Hawke's achievements were not enough to contain the ambitions of Paul Keating. He had been a reluctant recruit to the Hawke cause in

1983 because, even then, at age 38, he had plans to succeed Bill Hayden. Hawke and Keating had proven to be an effective combination, with the former the popular leader and steadying hand and Keating the driving force behind the Hawke Government's economic reforms. Keating told colleagues and supporters that he was "the real prime minister" and his impatience steadily grew, boiling over on occasions into threats to resign and take "the Paris option". There were strong differences between the two, mostly argued out behind closed doors but periodically emerging in public, such as when Keating told a supposedly off-the-record Press Gallery dinner that Australia had not had any real leaders and that he was the Placido Domingo of Australian politics.

In November 1988, Hawke, with what he called "considerable reluctance", agreed to a demand from Keating for a commitment on the succession. Hawke saw it as a way of buying time and easing the relentless pressure from his rival. With Hawke's choice of businessman Sir Peter Abeles and Keating's choice of ACTU Secretary Bill Kelty as witnesses, they met at Kirribilli House, the Prime Minister's Sydney residence, where Hawke said he wanted to lead Labor at the next election and would then hand over the leadership to Keating during the following term. The agreement remained secret – it would have reduced Hawke to a lame duck if it had not – until Senator Graham Richardson, the Right's power broker, leaked it to Channel 9's Laurie Oakes, precipitating Keating's first leadership challenge in May 1991. That was after Hawke had made clear he would not honour the agreement, arguing that Keating had disqualified himself because of his behaviour, in particular Hawke's claim, denied by Keating, that he had told him that if he didn't get his "turn" as Prime Minister, "we'll be off to Europe; we won't be staying here – this is the arse-end of the world". Hawke wrote in his biography that "his comment about Australia will always stick in my craw. In the mysterious workings of political osmosis it goes a long way to explain why Australians will not take to a man who thinks so little of them and their country". Hawke argued that only he could win the next election – a claim Keating was to disprove in 1993.

Labor had never torn down a serving prime minister and to set a precedent with one who had won four elections was particularly audacious. On the other hand, Hawke had form: he had destabilised Bill Hayden in 1982, lost a leadership ballot but continued his campaign until Hayden resigned on the day Malcolm Fraser called the election. And he had struck an agreement with Keating to hand over the leadership. The Kirribilli agreement became the weapon to force Hawke's hand. In the party room ballot that followed Oakes broadcasting the story, Hawke prevailed by 66 votes to 44, with the Left, who had been Hawke's most vociferous critic even from before he entered Parliament, deciding as a faction to support him, though a few broke ranks. Keating went to the backbench, declaring that "I only had one shot in the locker and I fired it".

The denial of further ambition has become part of the ritual of leadership ballots but so has the second challenge. It came 6 months later when the Hawke Government without Keating failed to find an effective response to the recession and to Opposition Leader John Hewson's ambitious reform package that included a consumption tax and changes to Medicare. Hawke and the government had fallen well behind in the opinion polls; the weapon that Hawke had used against Hayden now was being turned against him. The Hawke Government stuck stubbornly to the tight Budget policy that the former Treasurer had designed, while Keating himself was performing one of his classic political pirouettes by arguing for more stimulus. As well, Keating's replacement as Treasurer, John Kerin, stumbled in the job and Keating and his supporters kept destabilising the government in a form of political water torture, eroding Hawke's authority drip by drip. In the second leadership ballot Keating prevailed by 56-51. Three more votes for Hawke and he would have survived but there was no second chance for the Prime Minister. Labor's most successful leader became the first Labor Prime Minister to be rejected by his party.

Life after politics

It was after his defeat that the wider public finally was exposed to Hawke's less attractive side. In 1994 he divorced Hazel and married d'Alpuget, who had been his lover on and off since the 1970s. Hazel, widely admired by the public for her strength and forbearance, died in 2013 after a long battle with Alzheimer's disease. According to Dementia Australia, she was the first prominent Australian to speak publicly about her illness and she established a fund to raise money for research and to provide services for sufferers and their carers.

Some of Hawke's public behaviour was crass. He was intent of making money by commercialising his political career. He resumed drinking and gambling, sometimes to excess. Though he had a reputation for not bearing grudges, he refused to forgive Keating and predicted, wrongly, that he would lose the 1993 election. *The Hawke Memoirs* were published in 1994, with much of the attention focused on his criticisms of Keating, who complained that the book was intended to personally vilify him.

Hawke embarked on a brief media career, interviewing prominent figure in Australia and abroad. He set up a business consultancy which traded on his connections, particularly in China. He played a leading part in setting up the Boao Forum, the Asian equivalent of the World Economic Forum that brings together political and business leaders and other opinion makers. The Bob Hawke Prime Ministerial Centre at the University of South Australia and the Hawke Research Institute engaged in a broad range of public policy issues.

Ever the conciliator, Hawke set up the International Centre for Muslim and non-Muslim Understanding at the University of South Australia. "I am convinced that one of the great potential dangers confronting the world is the lack of understanding in regard to the Muslim world", he said in 2004. "Fanatics have misrepresented what Islam is. They give a false impression of the essential nature of Islam. There are also fanatical Jews and Christians. They do no justice to the religions they claim to represent and in the process engender hatred that leads to war".

Freed from the constraints of office, he also took on some controversial causes. He was an advocate for nuclear power as a means of tackling climate change, as well as arguing that Australia should take advantage of its stable geology and generate substantial income by offering to store the nuclear waste of other countries. He supported euthanasia, describing as absurd "a position where a person is in terrible pain and for some quasi-religious or moral reason you're going to make them suffer and suffer and suffer". And he added that if he were ever to "lose his marbles", he would want his wife to end his life with the help of their GP.

Hawke died peacefully at his Sydney home on May 16, 2019, two days before the election that Labor under Bill Shorten was widely expected to win. Instead, Liberal Prime Minister Scott Morrison was re-elected, declaring that he had always believed in miracles.

Conclusion

The Labor Party long harboured more doubts about Bob Hawke than the Australian people. As John Button put it in his letter to Bill Hayden in 1983, trying to persuade him to relinquish the leadership: "I must say that even some of Bob's closest supporters have doubts about his capacities to lead the party successfully, in that they do not share his own estimate of his ability". But he continued, Labor was desperate to win.

Hawke turned out to be a winner in four successive elections – two more than any previous Labor prime minister. He served as prime minister for eight years and nine months, a record beaten only by John Howard's 11 years and nine months and Robert Menzies' 18 years and five months (in two separate terms). He also turned out to be a leader of substance, ranking him alongside such figures as Alfred Deakin, John Curtin, Menzies, Gough Whitlam and Howard. The personality weaknesses he displayed in large relief – his drinking to excess, his temper, his serial infidelity – were sublimated to his ambition to lead the nation or hidden from public view.

No prime minister has matched him for the sheer volume of major reforms, particularly on the economy. Many of them had nothing to do with traditional Labor policy; indeed they directly contradicted it. Hawke and his Treasurer Paul Keating were always prepared to put pragmatism ahead of ideology. They governed in an internationally conservative era, with Ronald Reagan US President for most of Hawke's prime ministership and Margaret Thatcher UK Prime Minister for all but the last few weeks. The fashion was to give free rein to market forces.

Circumstances played a large role in his government's most significant economic decision – the floating of the dollar – which led almost inevitably to the other economic reforms of financial deregulation, cutting tariffs, labour market deregulation and privatisation. Nevertheless, implementing these reforms required political courage. A more timid government would have baulked and put them off for another day or a future government. Indeed, this was the criticism of the Fraser Government. Many of the changes were driven by Paul Keating as Treasurer but it was Hawke's public popularity and the political skills of both Hawke and Keating that navigated them through a resistant party and the three elections that followed the 1983 victory. The real secret to the success of his government was that Hawke built and preserved political capital, enabling Keating to spend it. But it was a daredevil ride. Labor lost votes, though not always seats, in every election after 1983 and the Government barely survived in 1987 and 1990. Still, given the extent of the reforms, which often were unpopular and for which the government could not claim a mandate, it is surprising it did so well.

Neal Blewett, who was a minister for ten years in the Hawke and Keating governments, has written:

> ...it is difficult to see any Labor leader other than Hawke winning four consecutive elections, particularly given the economic turbulence of the 1980s and early 1990s. All this was achieved in an age when the West was dominated by libertarian philosophies and conservative political parties. For a Labor government to exist in such a climate, even if it did somewhat change its spots, was remarkable; that it survived for over a decade is extraordinary.

Blewett added that possibly Hawke's greatest achievement was to preside over profound changes that transformed the economy without any serious fracture in the ALP. Labor had split on three previous occasions on matters of ideology and policy – during World War One over conscription, during the 1930s over the economic policy response to the Great Depression and in the 1950s over Communism. On each occasion, the consequence was to keep Labor out of office for long periods.

The Hawke Government argued that the economic reforms were a means to an end: they resulted in a more productive economy that brought more prosperity to more people. The modern day critique of what is called neoliberalism is that it has brought greater inequality. The excesses of unbridled markets in Australia led to a severe recession at the end of the 1980s but it was followed by a long period of solid growth, with the economy benefiting from the increased productivity flowing from the Government's reforms.

As well, social policy initiatives tempered the trend to greater inequality. Medicare meant that free or cheap health care was available to Australians regardless of means. The family allowance supplement was foremost among the reforms in social security that supported children in families with low and middle income households. Other welfare reforms concentrated benefits to those most in need. Compulsory superannuation extended the coverage to all Australians, although the tax concessions accompanying it were skewed towards higher income earners. The 1986 tax reforms reduced, though did not eliminate, the opportunities for tax avoidance by higher income earners.

A note on sources

There is an extensive literature on the Hawke Government and I have drawn on it for much of the detail. This applies also to direct quotations: where not attributed directly in the text, in most cases they are drawn from the books, chapters and manuscripts listed in the Select Biography, apart from a few cases based on my interviews with contemporaries of Hawke. I also have relied on my own reporting and commentary of the period, including as Chief Political Correspondent for *The Sydney Morning Herald* from 1984 to 1988, when I encountered Hawke at close quarters, including on trips in Australia and overseas. I continued to write about the Government in subsequent positions as Political Editor and National Affairs Editor.

Select Bibliography

Blewett, Neal, 'Robert James Lee Hawke', in Michelle Grattan, (ed), *Australian Prime Ministers*, New Holland Publishers, Chatswood, 2001

Blewett, Neal, *A Cabinet Diary*, Wakefield Press, Kent Town, 1999

Bramston, Troy, *Bob Hawke, Demons and Destiny*, Viking, Ringwood, 2022.

D'Alpuget, Blanche, *Robert J. Hawke*, Schwartz, East Melbourne, 1982.

Edwards, John, *Keating, The Inside Story*, Viking, Ringwood, 1996.

Freudenberg, Graham, *A Certain Grandeur*, Macmillan, South Melbourne, 1977.

Hawke, Bob, *The Hawke Memoirs*, William Heinemann, Port Melbourne, 1994

Howard, John, *John Howard, Lazarus Rising*, HarperCollins, Sydney, 2010.

Kelly, Paul, *The Hawke Ascendancy*, Angus & Robertson, Sydney,1984.

Kelly, Paul, *The End of Certainty*, Allen & Unwin, St Leonards, 1992.

Richardson, Graham, *Whatever It Takes*, Bantam, Sydney, 1994.

Steketee, Mike, '*Labor in Power, 1983-96*', in John Faulkner and Stuart Macintyre, (eds), *True Believers, The Story of the Federal Parliamentary Labor Party*, Allen and Unwin, Crows Nest, 2001.

Steketee, Mike, unpublished obituary of Bob Hawke.

Steketee, Mike, *From Medibank to Medicare*, unpublished chapter.

Uren, Tom, *Straight Left*, Random House, Sydney, 1994.

Walsh, Peter, *Confessions of a Failed Finance Minister*, Random House, Sydney, 1995.